S0-BHZ-232

MANTEGNA

FRANCA ZAVA BOCCAZZI

GROSSET & DUNLAP
Publishers - New York

First American edition published by Grosset & Dunlap, Inc.
All rights reserved
Translated from the Italian by Pearl Sanders
Translation copyright © 1971 by Thames and Hudson, London
Copyright © 1969 by Sadea Editore, Firenze
Library of Congress Catalog Card Number: 70-110102

Printed and bound in Italy

Life

Andrea Mantegna was born in 1431, in the village of Isola di Cartura, which belonged to Vicenza. He was the son of Biagio, a carpenter. At a very early age, Andrea moved to Padua; the city's register of painters, covering the years 1441-5, lists his name as the adopted son of the artist Francesco Sparcione. The relationship between Mantegna and Squarcione was anything but serene; and, in 1448, when Mantegna was only seventeen, they even had to take their differences to the law.

This lawsuit took place in Venice, where Andrea had gone in company with Squarcione. Here he first came into contact with Venetian artistic circles, possibly already with Jacopo Bellini through a certain Ulisse d'Aliotti. D'Aliotti was one of the arbitrators in his dispute with Squarcione, and was on familiar terms with Bellini, having dedicated a sonnet to him in 1441, in honour of his victory over Pisanello in the competition for a portrait of Lionello d'Este.

By October 1448 Mantegna had already won financial independence, receiving payment for the quoin in Santa Sofia (forty ducats being paid to him by Master Bartolomeo, baker), and he was living in his own house in Venice, in the Paduan district of Santa Lucia; yet relations between him and Squarcione, unfriendly as they were, did not cease until 1456 with the final annulment of their lawsuit. Hostilities seemed to be continually renewed between them; once they led opposing factions in the judgment of some paintings (by Pietro di Milano, 5 September 1448); at another time Squarcione was given an opportunity to criticize Mantegna's work. He displayed ill-concealed malevolence in all sorts of petty squabbles and incitements; one instance of this took place on 15 February 1457 and concerned the number of Apostles in the Ovetari *Assumption*. Mantegna had reduced the number to eight for lack of space, but Master Francesco considered the space ample for twelve ' if they were painted smaller '.

Squarcione's relationship with his adopted son was thus not exactly a happy one; nor did Mantegna benefit very much from his teaching. But the adoptive surname stuck, and Andrea Mantegna was still called Squarcione in Pisa in 1467, where one of his panels was listed as the work of ' Andrea Squarcion '; a sonnet was dedicated to him as ' Andrea Mantinea pictore dicto Squarzono '. Mantegna's extraordinary precocity as a painter, which had already come to the public eye in 1448 with his altarpiece for Santa Sofia, was given official recognition in the same year when Madonna Imperatrice Ovetari commissioned him, on 16 May, to take part in the painting of the family chapel in the church of the Eremitani in Padua. According to the last will of her husband Antonio Ovetari, the chapel was to be decorated with the stories of St James and St Christopher, ' in a handsome and seemly manner '. His widow divided the work between two pairs of artists. One couple, Antonio Vivarini and Giovanni d'Alemagna, were already well-known and widely experienced; the other couple, Nicolò Pizzolo and Andrea Mantegna, were still beginners, but no less eager to excel. As things turned out, the Ovetaris were to favour the future rather than the past, the young Mantegna rather than his colleagues; the collaboration broke up with the death of Giovanni d'Alemagna, and the consequent withdrawal of Vivarini, in 1450, and the death of Pizzolo in 1453. Mantegna was left in charge. His artistic personality was gradually being revealed upon the walls of the chapel, and he became the focus of interest for all the most advanced artists in Northern Italy; fame and many commissions were to follow. In May 1449 he was summoned to Ferrara to paint the portrait of Lionello d'Este and of his favourite, Folco da Villafora (both now lost); on 21 July 1452, in Padua, he signed and dated the lunette over the great doorway showing St Antony and St Bernardine holding the monogram of Christ (now in the Museo Antoniano). The following year he began the polyptych of St Luke for the monks of Santa Giustina (finished in the autumn of 1454); also in 1454 he painted the *St Euphemia* now in the Museo Nazionale, Naples. During this period his activity in the

4

Ovetari chapel continued. He was joined there, in 1451, by Ansuino da Forlì and Bono di Ferrara, in place of Vivarini and D'Alemagna, the two Venetians who had been in charge of the right-hand wall. It is possible that Mantegna was still working in the chapel even after 1455, which is the last date of payment given in the most recently published documents.

Considering the amount of work he had on hand in Padua, it is difficult to imagine that Mantegna can have spent much time in Venice during those years. Fiocco maintains that he made the mosaic of the *Dormition of the Virgin* in the Mascolo Chapel in St Mark's, and the Cornaro monument in the church of the Frari, while he was there. He did marry in Venice however, in 1453, Nicolosia, daughter of Jacopo Bellini and sister of Gentile and Giovanni Bellini. This reinforced the relationship with the Bellini family which may have begun during Mantegna's first trip to Venice.

In Padua he continued to live in the district of Santa Lucia, and the years between 1456 and 1458 are minutely documented: we can follow him buying corn, pawning and redeeming a ring belonging to his wife Nicolosia (he worked hard but earned relatively little); and he almost certainly painted the canvas commissioned by the protonotary Gregorio Correr, abbot of San Zeno in Verona, in Padua at this time. This work occupied him from 1456 to 1459, according to the letters that were written by Marchese Ludovico Gonzaga, ruler of Mantua, to Correr and to Mantegna in 1457-9, in which he requested that Mantegna should come to Mantua, in fulfilment of an agreement made in 1457, as soon as the San Zeno paintings were finished. In these letters Gonzaga pleads and insists; he sends Luca Fancelli to persuade him, even prepares a schedule of work for him to do: the chapel of the castle, 'built in your style', is ready to be decorated; he promises to pay him a monthly salary, plus maintenance for six people, and to pay his travelling expenses. It appears that at one juncture in 1458, losing heart, he began to make plans (which did not however materialize) to take Michele d'Ungheria, known as Il Pannonio, to Mantua to fill

Mantegna's post. Mantegna may have completed one spell in Mantua during this time; in 1459 a certificate was issued to him by Ludovico in which he is named as being ' one of the household ' and giving him permission to use in his crest the motto PAR UN DÉSIR.

Certainly the San Zeno altarpiece is the only commission still extant belonging to this immediate period; however, we do know of a small work ordered by the mayor of Padua, Giacomo Antonio Marcello, since, on 14 March 1458, Gonzaga granted Mantegna ten days leave while he painted it (see note to *pl. 14*). However, the total volume of commission attributable to Mantegna's Paduan period is such that his hesitation about leaving the city seems fully justified; in 1458 he had engaged an assistant for six years. In 1460 he finally moved to Mantua. He was back in Padua again in 1461, but only passing through – he seems to have decorated the chimney breast of a house in the Santa Lucia district with a *Mourning for the son of Gattamelata*, now lost. Firmly established in Mantua, he at once began to work very hard, and his painting was highly esteemed by the artistic members of the court: the Veronese humanist Felice Feliciano, dedicating his collection of ancient inscriptions to him on 1 January 1463, called him ' prince of painters, most treasured of friends '.

During 1463 he was commissioned to decorate several of the Marchese's residences: he delegated the designs for the castle of Cavriano to Samuele da Tradate, but carried out the work at Goito himself; he was still at Goito in 1464, but was doing other work as well, possibly for the chapel of the palace in Mantua which had now been ready to paint for some time. In a letter written on 6 April, he mentions panels to be varnished and frames to gild, all of which, within the month, were to go into the chapel.

On 23 and 24 September 1464, Mantegna went on an archaeological tour of Lake Garda with Samuele da Tradate, Felice Feliciano and the architect Giovanni Antenore. Feliciano has left a curious description of the party. The four friends went off in search of Roman inscriptions and spent their time crowning each other with garlands, and giving each other Roman titles such as *Imperator* and

Consules. They worshipped at the *temple* of the Blessed Virgin, and prayed to ' the divine thunderer and his glorious mother ', in a semi-pagan, semi-Christian ritual which in some respects forecasts Mantegna's subsequent development. Meanwhile, the room in the Castello di San Giorgio in Mantua which was to become the Camera degli Sposi was being made ready. The date 16 June 1465 is scratched on a window squinch, but Mantegna did not arrive there until later (see notes to *pls 36-51*). He was in Florence on 5 July 1466, as we learn from a letter from Aldobrandini to Ludovico Gonzaga; he may have gone there to give advice on the architecture of the choir of Santissima Annunziata. He returned to Mantua at the end of the year, and went again to Tuscany in 1467 to give advice on the painting of the Campo Santo in Pisa; a feast was given there in his honour on 3 July.

The correspondence between Mantegna and Marchese Ludovico Gonzaga during the years that followed is instructive. The tone of the relationship between them grew more and more familiar as Ludovico's admiration and appreciation of his artist increased, and the correspondence affords an intimate view of life in a fifteenth-century court. Gonzaga did not find it inappropriate that Mantegna should turn to him to complain about the insulting behaviour of a neighbouring greengrocer and his vulgar wife – in fact he took the case up, and the quarrelsome greengrocer came off very badly: Ludovico declared that ' we hold Andrea's little toe more dear than a thousand such louts '. There was also a difference with a tailor over an ill-fitting overcoat; here the Marchese reserved judgment until he had checked the facts personally: ' I shall decide when I see the case on Monday.' He never appeared irritated by the artist's incessant complaints, although they were often unfounded (Aliprandi described Mantegna as ' such a cantankerous and disagreeable person that none of his neighbours can live at peace with him '). The Marchese wanted Mantegna's work, and in order to make sure of keeping him he handled him with great patience and wisdom. He not only answered his often insistent demands for money but also bore with his aspirations to nobility, awarding him the title of Count

Palatine which he coveted; Mantegna was to sign his name and title later on when working in the Vatican. Mantegna's familiarity with the court grew to such an extent that, in September 1472, after having complied with Cardinal Francesco's request to keep him company while he was taking a cure at the baths at Porretta, near Bologna, he invited the Cardinal to dine at his house – but not before having given the Marchese instructions about what game he would need: ' please deign to make sure that I have quails and a few pheasants as well '. The liberality of the prince encouraged Mantegna in this familiarity: he signs himself SUUS ANDREA on the frescoes in the Camera degli Sposi – a curious phenomenon for those times (they were finished in 1474).

Mantegna's position at court was made financially secure by endowments which allowed him to buy a smallholding at Buscaldo and possessions at Pradella, Aquadruccio and other places (these purchases were often turbulent transactions, and as usual the assistance of the Marchese was called upon); he built his house at San Sebastiano, finishing it in 1476, according to the inscription over the door; it was often visited by the Gonzaga family, and Lorenzo the Magnificent went there in 1483. Ludovico Gonzaga's son Federico, who succeeded his father in 1478, behaved just as considerately to Mantegna: he saw personally to the payment of the painter's salary, writing, the year after his succession, to his wife Margherita from the battlefield to instruct her to pay him; he made sure that the painter's sick son should be treated by the physician Gherardo da Verona. When Mantegna failed to requite this solicitude, as when, for example, he refused to copy ' certain sketches for paintings ' which the Duchess of Milan had asked the Marchese to send her, Federico found a tactful way of excusing him: ' These great masters have their whims, and one must be thankful for what one can get from them.'

Mantegna continued to be very active during these years, extending his field to architecture (he acted as artistic adviser to Giovanni Antenore at Marmirolo in 1481) and goldsmith's work (he designed scent jars and bottles for the goldsmith Gian Marco Vavalli in 1483). We do not know

8

exactly which of Mantegna's paintings is referred to as a Madonna 'with other figures', commissioned by Eleanor of Aragon, Duchess of Ferrara, which was being discussed avidly in 1485 not only by Federico but by Francesco Gonzaga and Bishop Ludovico Gonzaga as well. By the following summer Mantegna was already at work on *The Triumph of Caesar*, which was seen and admired by Ercole di Ferrara; it was not to be finished until after Mantegna's return from Rome.

After the marriage of his daughter Laura, whose dowry he finally paid in December 1486, Mantegna left for Rome with a letter of introduction to Pope Innocent VIII from Francesco Gonzaga (10 June 1488). He stayed there two years while he painted the private papal chapel at the Belvedere, later knocked down to make way for the Museo Pio Clementino; all that remains of the chapel are descriptions of it in writing (by Raphael Maffeus, Vasari and, in the eighteenth century, Taja and Chatard). Mantegna gives no description of it in his Roman correspondence, although he gives us a number of biting comments on Djem, brother of the Sultan of Turkey and prisoner of the Pope, and airs his worries about the conservation of the *Triumph* which he had begun in Mantua. One curious and characteristic anecdote is known, however: it seems that Mantegna added an eighth Deadly Sin to the usual seven, depicting Ingratitude, and alluding, as Mantegna himself explained, to the Pope's tightfistedness; he obviously compared very unfavourably with Mantegna's Mantuan patrons.

Mantegna returned to Mantua after an illness, in 1490, but not (if we are to believe Vasari) before he had started a scheme for making engravings from many of his paintings; not all the critics are agreed that he did any engraving himself (Tietze, for example, denies it), but nevertheless he certainly directed the work and imbued it with his own stylistic trade-marks. A decree by the Marchese Francesco, dated 14 February 1492, invested Mantegna with an estate to reward him for those paintings which were considered to be his greatest works: the decorations of the chapel, the Camera degli Sposi and the *Triumph of Caesar*, still unfinished but already extravagantly praised. Mantegna's son Francesco, who, with a team of collaborators, had begun a highly complex scheme of decorations at Marmirolo, was commissioned to paint there a replica of the *Triumph of Caesar*.

After the victory of Fornovo (6 June 1495) the votive chapel of Sant'Andrea was instituted, and the following summer the *Madonna della Vittoria* (now in the Louvre) was carried there in solemn procession from the painter's studio in San Sebastiano. The altarpiece painted for the monks of Santa Maria in Organo, in Verona, which is now in the museum of the Castello Sforzesco in Milan, bears the date 15 August 1497.

Mantegna had already started the allegorical paintings commissioned for the Studiolo in Mantua by Isabella d'Este, wife of Marchese Francesco, and by 3 July 1497 his *Parnassus* was already in place. Though now an old man, Mantegna continued to work until the very end of his life. His querulous complaints to the Marchese continued right to the end (he requested that his barber be punished for robbing him); his battle for his rights continued, and there were some disappointments – he had to hand over to Isabella a marble bust of the Empress Faustina which he loved very much and was very sad to be without.

He made his will on 17 March 1504, in favour of his three sons: Francesco, the painter; Ludovico, his favorite, who was chaplain to the Gonzaga family at Cavriana; and his illegitimate son Gianandrea. Two hundred ducats were set aside for his chantry in Sant'Andrea. He collapsed with a stroke at the end of 1505, but went back to work again, according to a letter from him to Isabella, on 13 January 1506; he started work on the *Legend of the god Comus* for the walls of the Studiolo, but it remained unfinished at his death on 13 September. He was buried in Sant'Andrea, and a very lively portrait head, which may be a self-portrait, stands as his monument.

Works

There has been a tendency for art historians evaluating Mantegna's cultural background to use a kind of circular reasoning – inferring the nature of his antecedents from the nature of his work, without establishing a causal link. The reason for this is probably the fact that Mantegna's painting, including even his earliest works, forms a coherent unity which can hardly be said to undergo any development: it is, from the start, the conscious expression of a mature artist. Artistic antecedents have been singled out from the figurative arts of the years immediately preceding 1450, where premonitions of his work are to be found. This method of enquiry, in which a cultural situation is assessed as a whole, has many advantages, but the role of intangible factors should not be overlooked. If, as is generally accepted, Andrea Mantegna is to be thought of as one of the most inspired interpreters of the spirit of the Renaissance (meaning by this that he introduced new spiritual values and fully developed his own aesthetic), to look back in time for the seeds of his work, or for facts relevant to his case, may be instructive from a historical point of view, but it is not an indispensable part of a full appreciation of the artist. He embodies a unique complex of characteristics derived largely from the strength of his own creative energy, and although there is no doubt that the arrival of Tuscan art in the Veneto brought with it all manner of new modes of thought, the communication between two civilizations and the real impulse towards a revision of values cannot be regarded as the solution to all the problems which surround the work of Mantegna. Nor is it very helpful to spend a great deal of time discussing Francesco Squarcione and whether the discovery of Mantegna was attributable to him or not, or indeed if he took any part in his education at all.

I do not want to enter into the dispute about the extent of Squarcione's influence; but in the work of Zoppo and Schiarone, to name only two of the most gifted of the 'one hundred and thirty-seven disciples' (Scardeone) who made up Squarcione's curious workshop, there is a consistency of vocabulary and style which displays certain of the marks of Venetian art of the fifteenth century. However, the relationship between this phenomenon and the painting of Mantegna (who had been a member of the group for a short time) could not, because of the profound difference between their aesthetic horizons, have gone beyond the basic techniques of painting and some common interests. The capricious and even eccentric 'temperament' that characterized Squarcione's followers was not Mantegna's; nor was their tortuous stylization, which was to develop, with the help of acquisitions from Mantegna's own territory, into the exquisite visionary painting of Cosimo Tura. As Fiocco has shown, the closest ancestors of Mantegna's *St Peter, St Paul* and *St Christopher*, in the Ovetari Chapel in Padua, are the frescoes in the chapel of San Tarasio, at San Zaccaria, by Andrea del Castagno, painted in 1442; Mantegna must have seen these during his first visit to Venice. They clearly also made a strong impression on Nicolò Pizzolo, to judge by his resplendent *God the Father*, his first exercise in the Eremitani with his young colleague.

The collaboration between Mantegna and Pizzolo, organized by Imperatrice Ovetari, who gave one half of the chapel to each painter, was not simply by chance: it gives us some indication of the circles in which Mantegna had chosen to move in the artistic milieu of Padua. Nicolò Pizzolo, painter and sculptor, had collaborated with Donatello in the bas-reliefs for the church of the Santo, and had worked with Ansuino da Forlì and Lippi in the lost frescoes of the chapel of the Podestà; he represented the new current of Tuscan influence in Padua. His premature death at the end of 1453 came before he had had time to finish his assignment in the Ovetari Chapel; his contributions were the *God the Father*, mentioned above, *St James*, the *Fathers of the Church* in the tondi of the apse, and the huge head on the right-hand side of the arch; these already showed signs of an individual style which married most happily with Mantegna's own parallel contribution. Mantegna carried on the work by himself, and the maturity of his thought and his style are really extraordinary; already strongly developed are the characteristics which he retained almost unchanged throughout his whole career as a painter. His vision is a synthesis of the cultural situation of which he was part, in all its complexity, resolved through his own creative sensibility.

It has been shown how many artistic innovations arrived from Tuscany with the arrival in the Veneto of many of the key figures of the Florentine Renaissance. The two Lamberti were in Venice in 1415-16; Paolo Uccello was in Venice from 1425, and then, from 1444, in Padua where he was joined after a year by Donatello. Filippo Lippi had been there since 1434. Andrea del Castagno signed his frescoes in San Zaccaria in 1443. Dello Delli was in the Veneto between 1427 and 1433. The new ideas that they brought with them were based on new modes of critical investigation, of a scientific as well as an artistic nature: objective reality had been rationalized and had found new applications, both in the choice of subject matter and in the formal structure of paintings. The Florentines found in Padua a highly sophisticated cultural climate, which suited them, and there grew up a centre of humanism which was second only to Florence in the quality of its achievements. Padua was, perhaps, even keener than Florence in its dedication to the rediscovery of antiquity and the evocation of the past – both of which were already traditionally rooted in Venetian minds.

It is probably true to say that it was in the case of Mantegna that these two different civilizations achieved their most harmonious union, a sudden fusion of spiritual certainty and poetic realism. This realism is wonderfully expressed in the Ovetari Chapel: completely fresh and new, yet receptive to new stimuli – welcoming the influence of Castagno, Uccello, Donatello. The old ways of thought are incorporated too, but their freshness is revived in a new narrative context which may owe something to the experiments of Jacopo Bellini. Mantegna's realism is tinged with official contemporary culture, with scientific positivism and naturalism, and of course with the erudition of the huma-

13

nists. Scholars have detected the echo of the teachings of Mussato and Gasparino Barzizza, and glimpsed the influence of the Greek Emmanuel Chrysoloras, of Guerrino da Verona, Francesco Filelfo, Vittorino da Feltre and many others. The most novel and perhaps most exciting of the influences to be traced in Mantegna's figurative imagination made the most profound impression on his taste and on his very way of life: this was the impulse that sent Marcanova on his quest for Roman inscriptions, which inspired the widespread passion for archaeology and for the collection of antiquities. These antiquities, and the relics which littered Squarcione's studio, were the direct sources of Mantegna's personal vision of classical antiquity. His vision was also coloured by his lucid appreciation of the painting of Piero della Francesco and Roger van der Weyden; Mantegna encountered both artists during his sojourn in Ferrara, when he was summoned to the d'Este court in 1449 to paint the portraits of Lionello and his favourite. This began the relationship with Ferrara which was to continue with his collaboration in the Ovetari Chapel with Ansuino da Forlì and Bono da Ferrara, and which finally ended during the second half of the century with Mantegna's own major contribution to Ferrarese culture.

The attempt to trace not only an order of work in the Ovetari Chapel (this was partially documented anyway) but also a parallel stylistic progression, using the various cultural stimuli noted above as a guide, is a legitimate critical undertaking but a difficult one; the inherent difficulties are aggravated by the fact that it is almost impossible to estimate at what time during the five years, which we know were spent on the chapel, Mantegna came across each influence, and when he used it in his work. It is thought that the two first episodes in the St James cycle, in the upper lunettes of the left-hand wall, followed his visit to Ferrara in May 1449. It is immediately obvious how far removed the dignified figures and the limpid, semi-tangible space are from the rough, heavy forms crowded together in the airless landscape of the *Calling of St James*, or the disorganized drama of the astounded figures in *St James addressing the demons*. The tortuous expressiveness of these two pictures anticipates Mantegna's long predilection for 'geological' landscapes and his propensity for strewing his scenes with portions of buildings in the Renaissance classical manner.

It has been proved conclusively that the *Assumption (pl. 1)* was painted between 1454 and 1457, but the chronology of the six episodes of the St James cycle, that is the chronology of the whole left-hand wall, and the two additional episodes of the St Christopher cycle in the lower portion of the right-hand wall, poses a problem that has yet to be finally resolved. Although early historians and some modern critics consider these episodes in the *Life of St Christopher (pls 2-3)* to be the last of Mantegna's works in the Ovetari Chapel, another, just as authoritative, body of scholars places them somewhat earlier because of the difference in style between them and the episodes which face them, and because of the lack of rapport between the St Christopher episodes and any of the other paintings by Mantegna in the chapel. Without attempting to provide a solution, I should like to point out that the very obvious uniqueness of the episodes might be intentional, to place them outside the cycle; or they might represent a new stylistic departure, in which case their lack of influence on the rest of the paintings would suggest that they were painted last. Nor can I find in them any harshness of thought or expression, or any lack of maturity, which might detract from the elegant and spacious composition of the whole.

The architecture does not seem monumental, yet it has involved considerable structural ingenuity on the painter's part. The arrangement of the perspective does not stop at the creation of a single central point of view; Mantegna proposes a second focus for the participation of the spectator, bringing him into direct communication with the figures leaning out of the large window on the first floor to watch the incident: this idea of spectators at a performance, suggested in the San Zeno altarpiece, was to be fully exploited in the Camera degli Sposi. The colour, though substantially renovated, has none of the raw quality which it has in the other episodes; the figures are exceptionally human and have the naturalness and wit of real portraits: according to Vasari, the lifelike characters were painted after Squarcione's criticisms of the earlier set 'who were no good because they had been painted in imitation of antique marble sculptures'. All the elements of this painting suggest that this was the period at which Mantegna was most influenced by Tuscan models; as Ragghianti surmises, he may well have been thinking of the scenes with giants, now lost, painted by Paolo Uccello in the courtyard of the nearby Casa Vitaliani; Mantegna (as Campagnola also mentions) 'was greatly impressed' by them. It is strange that the painting of the St Christopher scenes should coincide with, or come just after, the first episodes of the St James cycle, in many ways opposite to them in style and conception: the early St James stories are really clumsy and crude, but the figures that appear in them recur throughout the whole cycle, and develop gradually, growing more and more controlled, though not changing fundamentally at all. It is quite possible that Mantegna painted all the episodes of the *Life of St James* from start to finish, breaking off to attend to other commissions; he had after all been commissioned to do just that, with the exception of *The Martyrdom of St James*, assigned to Pizzolo but completed by Mantegna after his death. In fact, Pietro di Milano mentions them, praising them, together with *The Assumption*, in his judgment of all those of Mantegna's paintings which were completed by 13 February 1457. The *Life of St Christopher* is not mentioned.

It is still not known which pieces of work are referred to in the payment made to Mantegna in 1451, but it is worth remembering that in the same year Bono da Ferrara and Ansuino da Forlì were also paid; Ansuino da Forlì in that same year signed his *St Christopher preaching*, which was patently inspired by Mantegna's *Baptism of Hermogenes* on the opposite wall. Here for the first time Mantegna has constructed a setting based on the canons of perspective laid down by Leone Battista Alberti, placing his figures on a paved surface. The figures are elongated in proportion, and may be derived from Jacopo Bellini. Archaeology, or rather the evocation of the classical world in sentimental terms by a romantic Paduan in love with antiquity, appears in the adjoining *St James before Herod Agrippa*: the Roman triumphal arch may be a deliberate copy of the Arch of Constantine, particularly as a bas-relief of the Sacrifice appears on the left-hand side; the Roman inscription is one listed by Macanova in Monte Buso, near Este, which was also reproduced by Jacopo Bellini in his notebook, now in the Louvre. Other inscriptions, more or less authentic, are to be found in *St James led to his martyrdom* and the left-hand episode in the *Life of St Christopher*. The extent of Mantegna's debt to his father-in-law can be estimated by looking at the albums of drawings in the Louvre and in the British Museum; it is also apparent in his predilection for rocky landscapes with wayfarers climbing up winding, cobbled paths (these were to become an important part of Mantegna's repertory); in his use of decorative medallions based on the designs of Roman coins, and his cities of strange buildings, bristling with towers and pinnacles, standing enclosed by battlemented walls at the very top of a hill.

It is possible that at about this time Mantegna painted the violent giant head on the left-hand side of the arch, which may be a self-portrait. I prefer to place it a little later, at the moment when, after a long pause while he was otherwise employed, he painted *The Assumption* and the last episodes of the St James cycle. The interruption of the work in the chapel between 1452 and 1454 produced quite a lot of work elsewhere, if we accept the extension of Mantegna's Paduan catalogue, documented in three cases: it produced the frescoed lunette over the main entrance to the church of the Santo which has disappeared under restorations and repaintings (Pietro Liberi repainted the head of St Antony); the Naples *St Euphemia* in 1454 – the saint stands dignified and worldly in her jewels and curls, filling a whole archway which is adorned by a festive garland of fruit which appears again in the San Zeno altarpiece; lastly, the *St Luke polyptych*, completed between 1453 and 1454 (*pls 4-7*). The lower edge of the *St Luke polyptych* was originally a straight line, but has been altered by the modern frame which does not match the original one; the original intention was to have a kind of perspective platform, foreshortened by a lowered point of vision – as is to be found in the Ovetari chapel and in the Verona canvas. This eye-level perspective gives a sense of spatial realism which is not disturbed by the flat gilded background. The saints stand with great dignity within this space, their robes brushing the marble edge of the platform and their bodies all slightly turned towards the middle. Each figure is constructed with great expressive energy and what seems to be a new moral force; each is stylistically perfect and extraordinarily graceful. St Justina, exquisite with her pink robe and her gentle face, has the same rapt intensity as the Virgin in the Ovetari *Assumption*. In the central compartment of the lower tier, set back a little from the apparent position of the other figures, stands a low dais which supports a huge St Luke behind a massive writing-desk. This is seen in great detail: the rough wood fresh from the saw, bottles of black and red ink, brilliant crimson bookmarks. The composition is planned with the most lucid comprehension of order and space in their Renaissance significance; mankind has gained heroism and responsibility. All that remains of the past is the gold background, the Gothic compartments in which the figures stand, and the hierarchy reflected in the relative sizes of the figures themselves.

When Mantegna painted the *Assumption* and the final episodes of the St James cycle in the Ovetari Chapel, he had already begun his experiments with perspective. He goes on experimenting to the point of exaggeration, projecting figures upwards in the most daring fashion as if they had been hoisted up in front of the spectator. He even makes use of this device in scenes which are supposed to be happening below the person looking at them. It is as if the painter, fascinated by his new and daring experiments, had decided to ignore the spectator. His lack of interest in the logical observer-image relationship is already manifest in the *Assumption*, where the figure of the Virgin (*pl. 1*) rises up from the level of vision, but the figures of the apostles below are seen from a position appreciably lower still: this is in fact intentional and absolutely original, giving the painting extraordinary power. Mantegna exploited the same device to its limit in *St James led to martyrdom*, which followed immediately afterwards.

In this scene the eye is drawn inescapably towards the back, around the great classical arch and the bleak buildings of the city street. The heavy, stony figures are enlivened by a breath of heroism and humanity in their moment of intense drama. Since painting the scenes described above, Mantegna had refined his thought and his style, and had discovered the direction in which he was moving; at the same time this work reveals the persistence of aspirations which are still Gothic. The path he has chosen to follow carries with it the danger of rejecting the rationalized objectivity of space and of the representation of mankind which are vital adjuncts to any art which is to flourish in the spirit of the Renaissance: Mantegna recovers these adjuncts, however, when he reverts to the open-air world of the Tuscan painters and of Piero della Francesca in the last two of the St Christopher episodes. This recovery begins to be noticeable in the clear and sparkling air of the *Martyrdom of St James* (see p. 20). There is a bald hill, dotted with trees and crowned with the classical ruins and medieval towers which are so much a part of Mantegna's landscape vocabulary; the figures are calm and free from drama, seeming almost indifferent to the killing which is taking place in the foreground.

The many different experiments to be found in the Ovetari frescoes could be said to be summed up in the *San Zeno altarpiece*, which was completed in 1456 when Mantegna was still occupied with the last of the frescoes. Some years before he began the altarpiece he must have finished the *Nativity*, now in New York, which still shows traces of northern naturalism in the manner of Van der Weyden ' in the caricature quality of the ragged peasants ' (Fiocco). The *St Jerome* in São Paulo, Brazil, definitely by Mantegna, shows the same traces, particularly in the style of the countryside and the composition of the rocky setting.

The amount of time spent by Mantegna on the *San Zeno altarpiece (pls 14-24)* gives some indication of the importance it held in the eyes of the painter; despite all Gonzaga's pleas, he put off his departure for Mantua in order to stay in Padua and finish it. This, then, was the painting that he intended to leave in the Veneto as his artistic testimony and

The Martyrdom of St James (see p. 30)

profession of faith; this fact gives us some clue to the thought, the self-inquiry and the minute examination of his own style and technique which went into it; it was to have the most profound influence on all subsequent painting in Verona. His interpretations are new and original, though he makes an open declaration of his sympathy with Donatello, linking his theme and some of the decorative work with the altarpiece in the church of the Santo.

In order that the altarpiece should be installed in the choir of San Zeno with appropriate dignity, it appears that Mantegna made the arrangements himself, helping to reorganize the presbytery and designing a window to be placed on the right of the painting, casting natural light on it to match the light already in the painting. The design for the frame, which is such an important part of the composition, was Mantegna's own: the four real half-columns give the false impression that the painting is divided into three different scenes (the term triptych is a misnomer) and form an indispensable part of the scenario; they are in fact architectural elements of the loggia in which the scene is set. The spatial structure of the painting does not stop inside the roof of the portico but extends on all four sides; the atmosphere surrounding the portico seems thin, ascetic, too rarefied to breathe; this is the atmosphere in which the spectator is standing, automatically transported into a surreal experience. The possibility of communication beween the interior and exterior space depends on the degree to which the spectator will participate: it involves a social as well as an architectonic consciousness. Mantegna had experimented with this idea in the final episodes in the St Christopher cycle, but here he has resolved it with the finality and certainty of a theorem. The composition is governed by a mathematical law which must be obeyed; each element is an inseparable part of the whole system, and has been so created by a clear desire for perfect order. The human forms are captured in immutable rhythms, and are as if hewn from precious stones in brilliant acid colours, enhanced by discordant contrasts. The same apparent incorruptibility affects the sumptuous festoons of fruit, which were so much a part of the Paduan artistic vocabulary and particularly appreciated in all their opulence by Mantegna; here they are suspended from the marble architraves by horns of purest coral. The profusion of decoration and the multiplicity of formal designs do not detract from the stylistic unity of the whole; in fact they accentuate the coherence and carefully planned proportions of the painting.

In the three parts of the predella, unfortunately now divided between Paris and Tours, Mantegna reveals with great vivacity and immediacy the realm where his most genuine feelings lie, giving us some idea of his personal poetics. Men and objects are portrayed without sentiment; spectral scenery awaits the arrival of the human being, enclosed in the painful silence of apathy, the suffering of a wordless

21

cry of anguish. In the bleak *Crucifixion* in the Louvre (*pls 21-3*) the Roman soldiers playing at dice are no less mournful than the group surrounding Mary and the group of apostles, or even the rough hedge of rocks along the road leading through the bleak houses of Jerusalem, crowded between their turreted walls. In the *Resurrection* in Tours (*pl. 24*) the setting is natural and very bare, in spite of a few cedar trees here and there. The sad, silent figure of Christ seems to be hewn from the same material as his sepulchre; sad too are the apostles in their uncomfortable positions. The jewel-like colours of the San Zeno predella, raw and bright (particularly in *The Crucifixion*) are repeated with much greater variety of light and shade in *The Crucifixion* which is now in London; this certainly belongs to the same period, sharing the same basic idea and certain obvious stylistic ties. There are ties as well with the *St Sebastian* in Vienna (*pls 10-11*) which is signed, with a humanistic pride, in Greek characters; here the feeling for landscape resembles that of the San Zeno altarpiece, and there is the same careful planning and complex decoration, but it stands apart, as does the *St Sebastian* (*pls 34-5*) in the Louvre (painted somewhat later and with greater emphasis on suffering), because of the inclusion of the architectural remains scattered around on the ground, and the broken arch used to support the figure of the Roman saint in his agony. These remains demonstrate the rediscovery of the classical heritage, so dear to the fifteenth-century humanists; Mantegna here exemplifies his personal, romantic evocation of antiquity, based on glimpses of the classical past but largely re-invented in mythical terms and with a visionary fervour which invests humanity with the incorruptibility of marble; his dream of the classical world is realized, formally and ideologically, in terms which are quite antithetical to classicism. He pursues his dream with the utmost enthusiasm, visually and intellectually, and it leads him to the formation of a new concept of space: what remained of his Tuscan heritage is exchanged for a new sense of perspective and a new set of plastic values.

Mantegna's move from Padua to Mantua was, as I see it, a victorious departure and not a defection or a renunciation;

it was fully justified by the good prospects of work in Mantua. As a young man Mantegna had witnessed Antonio Vivarini departing from Padua for the same reasons in 1450. It was not only awareness of his own needs that caused Mantegna's withdrawal from the artistic milieu of Padua: he was also well aware of the incompatibility between his poetics and the poetics of other painters who were coming to the fore. Giovanni Bellini, who embodied the whole future of Venetian painting, was beginning to develop what he had originally borrowed from Mantegna, opening new doors on to the truth about mankind and nature, and using new, intense colours: the two painters' respective *Agonies in the Garden*, both now in London, provide a perfect illustration of the disparity between these two great brothers-in-law.

The sum of Mantegna's achievements during the subsequent years in Mantua can be found in the Camera degli Sposi and the *Triumph of Caesar*; these are works of capital importance in the painter's career, and they were the focus of years of activity. Study of this activity may reveal an intermittent flagging in Mantegna's inventive powers (symptomatic in the allegorical paintings done for Isabella d'Este), but it does not reveal any basic changes in his stylistic and formal repertory: his language was mature and had ceased to develop before he left Padua, and for this reason it is not productive to search for new keys to the general critical understanding of the artist in his Mantuan paintings. The only objective way of applying some chronological order to an art which does not evolve is to base it on documentary sources: but as most documentary sources dealing with the late 1470s, when the Camera degli Sposi was finished, have disappeared, the work of the critical historian is made even more difficult. The attempts to trace the lost paintings of the palace chapel in order to assign a time and place to the *Triptych* in the Uffizi (*pls 27-30*) have not really been successful. Nor are there any documents to support Fiocco's hypothesis, which is in many ways an attractive one, that the three exquisite paintings were done during the artist's stay in Florence. Ideas already expressed in the San Zeno predella reappear in this triptych: landscape

23

details and decorative touches are very similar, and have the same brilliant colouring, though it is much more delicate in the *Circumcision*, which is not particularly closely linked with the other two panels. Longhi has suggested that *The Circumcision* is in fact the pendant of the *Death of the Virgin* (*pls 31-33*) in Madrid – they are even identical in size. If, as is probable, this was immediately followed by the *St George* in the Accademia in Venice (*pl. 33*), a tall, proud figure standing in the open window against an airy landscape, then it is possible that Mantegna was concentrating on small paintings during this period: he had the faculty of accommodating large subjects in very small paintings. The same faculty is manifest in the minute but monumental *Madonna and Child*, also placed by Fiocco during Mantegna's stay in Florence, but which I should place somewhat later, at the end of the 1480s, during his stay in Rome.

The Camera degli Sposi (*pls 36-51*) represents Mantegna's most impressive conquest over space, and exerted a profound influence over Correggio, Giulio Romano, Paolo Veronese and others right up to the baroque period; its novelty does not lie in the inclusion of the spectator as protagonist in the picture – this had already been tried in the *Life of St Christopher* and the San Zeno altarpiece. The new departure here is the placing of the convergent point of the perspective on a spot precisely in the centre of the square chamber. In the most straightforward way the spectator is directly involved in the pictorial action within and without the pavilion, decorated so richly with classical designs and carvings. Never before had *trompe-l'œil* on such a scale been attempted: the spectator is physically a part of the room, and of the countryside on to which it opens, and of the life of the characters. Their life is glimpsed at a certain moment and set down, and the figures have the immediacy of portraits. But their feelings are less clear and apprehensible: we seem to be studying a collection of very reserved personages, each one enclosed behind a mask conveying perfectly dignified apathy – contemporary heroes viewed with a slightly surrealistic eye; and their mythical aura embraces the vast sweep of landscape behind. Here, at some distance, Mantegna's wildest archaeological dreams have caused the most improbable township to be placed, a classical composition from the depths of his imagination.

So steeped was Mantegna in his private dream of antiquity that not even a visit to Rome and a sight of genuine classical remains could change him. He arrived in Rome in 1488, when the *Triumph of Caesar* had already been begun, and it is possible that its overall composition as a kind of Roman epic had already been sketched in. When he left Rome he left behind him the extremely elaborate and ornate decoration in the Vatican chapel; if we are to believe the historians it can have borne little relation to work begun in Mantua.

In the *Triumph of Caesar* (see p. 37), all Mantegna's experiments with perspective and space are summed up; but a new climate which already seems to belong to the sixteenth century affects his boldest foreshortening, and the vertical Gothic rhythms found in the Ovetari frescoes have gone. *The Triumph* is a horizontal procession, carefully planned so that the eye can move along it and take in the whole. The action proceeds very slowly, and is divisible into a series of sequences, and this gives the work a sense of movement which is rarely found in Mantegna's painting; the crowd of Romans in the train of the triumphal car, and the curious collection of bric-à-brac they carry with them, lack the usual marmoreal quality of Mantegna's figures.

The last ten years of Mantegna's life were years of intense activity and it is difficult to isolate in the work done during this time any fundamental variations in his expressive range or in his interests. He never participated in that search for a new relationship between the individual and the cosmos which was growing up early in the sixteenth century. The *Virgin and Child with cherubim* (*pl. 53*) probably also dates from 1485; reflections of Bellini are very noticeable in the gentleness of the head and the muted colours. The spherical heads of the little angels, characteristically modelled from all different angles, float on an untypically soft, cotton-wool cloud. The *Madonna della Vittoria* (*pls 54-7*) certainly dates from 1496; here the apse is constructed from the pleached branches of a tree, laden with precious fruits; brightness pours in from the right-hand side illuminating the spray of coral hanging from the dome and the powerful block of kneeling figures. In the *Virgin and Child with cherubim, saints and angels* (*pls 59-60*) in the Castello Sforzesco, Milan, the hanging scenery of boughs laden with gleaming apples and citrus fruits emphasizes the Gothic symmetry of the composition: Mantegna enhances the vertical lines by his foreshortening of the figures of the four saints, four grave and dignified personages undistracted by the concert of angels playing the organ.

Mantegna did not abandon his attachment to a certain style and content when very different subjects were required from him, such as the mythological scenes (*pls 66-79*), commissioned by Isabella d'Este between 1497 and 1502. He substituted pagan legend for the classical world, or, more precisely, mythology for archaeology, and he stuck to his intellectual symbolism and his favourite man-nature relationship. Nevertheless, there is a slight softening of the atmosphere, new flights of imaginative landscape and, particularly in the *Parnassus*, a literary type of mannerism. There may be premonitions of Poussin to be found in these scenes, but on the whole they come dangerously close to dull academicism. They represent, however, only one facet of the work of Mantegna's later years; another, more lively facet is demonstrated in the paintings found in his studio at the time of his death: the *Dead Christ* in the Brera (*pls 62-3*), *St Sebastian* (*pl. 64*) in the Ca' d'Oro in Venice, and the *Triumph of Scipio*, a final expression of Mantegna's lifelong fascination with Roman marble sculpture, painted, like the *Samson and Delilah* in London, in imitation of a classical bas-relief.

It is not absolutely certain that the *Dead Christ* and *St Sebastian* were in fact Mantegna's last works and, perhaps correctly, they have been dated at the end of the century. The livid *Dead Christ* (*pls 62-3*) transcends the sleight of hand needed to attempt so daring a piece of perspective to provide real intensity of expression, and could have been painted at an earlier stage in the artist's career; *St Sebastian* (*pl. 64*) is a truly conclusive work, at once a sum of the painter's mind and his technique. The figure is tragically imprisoned in his alcove, sublimely heroic, the contortions

St James healing a cripple (see p. 30)

of line reaching metaphysical proportions. It is interesting to consider *St Sebastian* together with the *Christ seated on a sarcophagus,* (*pl. 61*), in Copenhagen, which resembles it in the violently contracted face and the agonized twists of the white drapery, and discover how much of the Gothic there still remains; also, looking ahead, to remember how feeling will triumph over reason once again in the sixteenth century.

Mantegna and the critics

Many of the remarks made by sixteenth-century critics about Mantegna's treatment of perspective and the novelty and boldness of his foreshortening are still valid today (Santi, *Cronaca,* 1485; Leonardi, 1502; Serlio, 1537; Biondo, 1549; Daniele Barbaro, *La pratica della prospettiva,* 1569; Lomazzo, *Trattato dell'arte della pittura,* 1584, and *Idea del Tempio della pittura,* 1590). His ability to ' foreshorten figures seen from below ' was also admired by Vasari in both editions of the *Lives* (1550 and 1568). Vasari nevertheless found his invention somewhat over-sophisticated and criticized his tendency to concentrate on harshness and suffering and his ' somewhat dry manner '. Vasari's historical notes, vague and imprecise in the first edition, are based in the second on a letter from Girolamo Campagnola to the philosopher Nicolò Leonico Tomeo, that is to say on a direct contemporary source, and the information given coincides with that given by Scardeone (*De antiquitate urbis Patavii,* Basle 1560).

The comprehension and appreciation of Mantegna declined during the seventeenth century (Ridolfi, 1648; Scaramuccia, 1674), and it was not until the end of the eighteenth century that Lanzi made a contribution in his favour (1789). Mantegna as a personality was not studied in any depth until the end of the nineteenth century, by Cavalcaselle (*A History of Painting in North Italy,* 1871) and Berenson (*North Italian Painters,* 1897); both of these interpreted Mantegna's romantic evocation of antiquity as a deliberate ' Romanization ', and by implication accused him of narrowness of vision and circumscribed figurative taste. The first monographs on Mantegna, by Kristeller and Yriarte, both published in 1901, were less biased. In 1903 Eisler's article appeared (' Mantegna's frühe Werke und die römische Antike ' in *Monatsberichte für Kunst und Kunstwissenschaft*); Knapp's study appeared in 1910, and in 1914 Venturi published his *Storia dell'Arte Italiana,* which contains a substantial chapter on Mantegna. The greatest praise is due to Fiocco for his devoted revival of Mantegna studies and his acute appraisal of Mantegna's character. In his *Arte di Andrea Mantegna*, 1926, Fiocco concentrates in particular on the Paduan period and shows how it is linked with the culture of Renaissance Tuscany, imported into the Veneto in the early fifteenth century by Florentine artists. In his monograph of 1937 he puts forward his own general thesis which is helpful in clearing up many small details of Mantegna's life. In his *Cappella Ovetari*, 1953, he attempts to recover, with beautiful photographs and text, the youthful masterpiece now tragically lost. The lesser contributions of Longhi ('Risarcimento di un Mantegna', in *Pan*, 1934) and Ragghianti ('Casa Vitalani', in *Critica d'Arte*, 1937) are just as illuminating, about specific aspects of Mantegna's art, as is Tietze-Conrat's monograph published in 1955; in 1956 Renata Cipriani's short book entitled *Tutta la pittura di Andrea Mantegna* appeared. Certain documents have been published which are of great value historically: those referring to Mantegna's Paduan period were published by Lazzarini in *Nuovo archivio veneto*, 1908, Rigoni in *Atti del R. Istituto veneto di Scienze, Lettere ed Arti*, 1927-8, and in *Arte Veneta*, 1948; those dealing with the Mantuan period by Gerola (1908-9) and Luzio (1931 and 1940). In lectures given at the University of Padua during the academic year 1956-7 Pallucchini gives new insight into Mantegna's life and work, presenting it firmly in the context of fifteenth-century Venetian painting. In 1959 the valuable work by L. Coletti and E. Camesasca on the Camera degli Sposi appeared. An imposing exhibition of Mantegna's paintings was mounted in Mantua in 1961, and a catalogue with exhaustive notes was provided by Paccagnini. The exhibition gave rise to a general revival of interest in Mantegna and the discussion of various problems connected with his work in articles by Bottari (in *Arte Veneta*, 1961), Castelfranco (in *Bollettino d'Arte*, 1926) and Mellini Quintavalle and Ragghianti (in *Critica d'Arte*, 1962).

Notes on the Plates

The Ovetari Chapel. (See *pls 1-3*, illustrations on pp. 20 and 27.) Frescoes. Padua, Chiesa degli Eremitani. Only the photographic records of Mantegna's first great commissioned work remain; the frescoes in the Ovetari Chapel were destroyed in the bombardment of Padua on 11 March 1944, except for *The Assumption* (*pl. 1*) and *The Martyrdom of St Christopher* (*pls 2-3*), which had become detached from the wall over the years and, fortunately, had been sent away for restoration. As early as 5 January 1443 Antonio Ovetari had laid aside a legacy of 700 ducats for the decoration of the chapel, and the contract agreed on 16 May 1448 by his widow Madonna Imperatrice entrusted half the work to the painters Nicolò Pizzolo and Andrea Mantegna, the other half to Antonio Vivarini and Giovanni d'Alemagna. The programme was not carried out as planned because when Giovanni d'Alemagna died in 1450 Vivarini abandoned his share which was only partially done; and at the end of 1453 Mantegna had to take over Pizzolo's work because he, also, had died. Many studies have been published on the subject of the authorship of each part of the frescoes (Lazzarini, 1908; E. Rigoni, 1928 and 1948) and the matter has been more or less definitively cleared up: particularly since it is now certain that part of the right-hand wall is attributable to Ansuino da Forlì and Bono da Ferrara (Rigoni, 1948). Of all the decoration, which completely covered the dome and walls of the chapel, it has been agreed that Mantegna did the *St Peter, St Paul and St Christopher* in the spandrels of the apse, the *Assumption* on the further wall of the apse, the whole of the left-hand wall with the Life of St James and the episodes of the St Christopher series on the lower half of the right-hand wall. The chronology of Mantegna's paintings is still problematic, in particular the date of *The Martyrdom of St Christopher*. This has become the focus of discussion because it involves the stylistic evolution of the painter; many critics are interested in the problem and they are divided into those who would date it late (with the support of all sorts of arguments and hypotheses) and those who favour a much earlier date. Before the most recent publication of documents by Rigoni we only possessed two dates for Mantegna's participation in the Ovetari chapel: 1449 for the saints in the apse, which he painted first of all (lawsuit reported by Francesco Morosini on 27 September, between Mantegna and Pizzolo), and 1457 for the termination of *The Assumption* in the apse and the *Life of St James* on the left-hand wall (judgment on the paintings of Mantegna by Pietro da Milano, 13 February). On the basis of these dates a scheme of dates had been composed, beginning with the saints in the apse, continuing with the gigantic head on the left of the arch, then the two first episodes of the St James cycle in the lunette and then (with intervals for other commissions in Padua) the remaining episodes on the left-hand wall; last of all the *Assumption.* The lower panels of the right-hand wall were considered to be the final work in the chapel, showing the consecutive episodes of the martyrdom, and the transportation of the body of St Christopher. This thesis was based on Vasari, who lists all the portraits of contemporary personalities among the figures in the *Life of St Christopher*, including the Hungarian humanist Bishop Janus Pannonio, who was in Padua between 1454 and 1457: he is the bishop who dedicated an ode in gratitude to Mantegna. The historical accuracy of Vasari's notes should not of course be taken for granted, and especially where they concern Mantegna they are inaccurate and vague in many cases. I think it should be stressed that the reference to the work in the Ovetari Chapel does not appear until the second edition of the *Lives,* and Vasari had based his statements, as he himself declares, on a letter in Latin (now lost) from Girolamo Campagnola to the philosopher Nicolò Leonico Tomeo: the source is in fact credible both because the writer lived in Padua and was a contemporary of Mantegna (1435-1522) and because the information coincides with what Scardeone wrote later, in 1560. The theory that the Life of St Christopher antedates the lower episodes of the St James cycle, proposed on stylistic grounds by Eisler in 1903, was not accepted by Fiocco (1926 and 1937), though it was strongly supported by Ragghianti (in *Critica d'Arte,* 1937) and followed by Tietze in 1955 and Pallucchini in 1956-57. The last three support Rigoni's conclusion (1948) which amongst other things suggested the possibility that certain payments made to Mantegna in February and October 1451 were in respect of those final episodes on the right-hand wall. However, Paccagnini's revised reading of the relevant documents (in *Atti del VI convegno intern. di studi sul Rinascimento,* ed. 1965) puts what seemed to be conclusive in doubt. Paccagnini reveals that the date 1455 does not refer to the end of the work but only to the payment of the monies: the 3,263 lire yielded by the sale of the farm is equal to 570 ducats and not the 700 named in Ovetari's will in 1443; the work had been divided up into portions and payment was based on the 700 ducats available. The calculations of 1455 must have been based on the fact that two and a half portions were still to be painted: these were almost certainly the last episodes of the St Christopher series, completed well after this date and paid for later. Pietro da Milano, producing evidence in favour of Mantegna, would certainly have mentioned them, if they had been finished, in the judgment of 1457. Seen in the light of this new evidence I think that this question is undeniably moving towards a solution. Even if we exclude possible stylistic development from the argument, as I have done, I think we can rule out the possibility that in 1451 Mantegna, Ansuino da Forlì and Bono da Ferrara were all working on the same wall. Even the measurements of the final episodes in the Life of St Christopher are different from those of the last episodes of the St James cycle on the opposite wall, and this makes it clear that Mantegna had to finish off his colleague's work in that year. It may have been the reduced portion of wall that was left over that persuaded Mantegna to try the new solution of two episodes of the same story together in a single scenario.

1 Assumption. Fresco, base 238 cm. Padua, Eremitani, Ovetari Chapel, upper apse wall. Pizzolo was commissioned to paint this but it was painted by Mantegna after 6 February 1454 and before 13 February 1457. When the fresco was detached from the wall in 1865 the proportions were altered, but the original size can be seen in a print by Francesco Novelli after a drawing by Luca Brida, where there is a blank space between the Apostles and the Assumption (Fiocco).

2-3 The Martyrdom of St Christopher, and the Removal of St Christopher's body. Detached fresco (base 691 cm). Padua, Eremitani, Ovetari chapel, right-hand wall. The fresco is badly damaged, and the figure of the saint is missing; the body originally stuck out in the front of the left-hand side, as can be seen in the small copy in the Musée Jacquemart-André, Paris. In the scene with the arrows on the left (not shown) the largest soldier may be a portrait of Squarcione (Vasari, after Campagnola) and the one next to him with his head raised a self-portrait of Mantegna.

4-7 St Luke Polyptych. Panel, 178×227 cm. Milan, Brera. Below: in the centre St Luke (*pls 4-5*); left, SS. Scholastica and Prosdocimus; right, SS. Benedict and Justina (*pl. 6*). Above: Christ (*pl. 7*) with the Virgin and St John; left, SS. Daniel and Jerome; right, SS. Augustine and Sebastian. Commissioned by the monks of Santa Giustina in Padua 10 August 1453 and completed before 18 November 1454 (date of the final payment of 50 ducats); it remained in the chapel of St Luke in Santa Giustina until 1797. The original frame was signed (wrongly, according to Scardeone) by Mantegna but was destroyed in the eighteenth century. It had been made by a Maestro Guglielmo, probably to Mantegna's own design, and he paid 21 ducats for it.

8 Presentation in the temple. Canvas, 67×86 cm. Gemäldegalerie Berlin-Dahlem. Formerly in the Gradenigo collection in Padua and then from the early nineteenth century in the Solly collection; it was considered by Morelli and A. Venturi to be a copy of a painting seen by Michiel in Casa Bembo in Padua, now in the Galleria Querini Stampalia, Venice. But this is now recognized as a copy by Giovanni Bellini of Mantegna's original, and the Berlin canvas has been unanimously declared genuine; Cavalcaselle had already identified it in 1871. The date of the painting is still controversial: Kristeller, Posse, Tietze and Cipriani attach it to the Paduan period; Fiocco to the beginning of the first Mantuan period; Gamba and Paccagnini to 1466 (in the Catalogue to the Mantegna exhibition); Berenson to the end of Mantegna's career.

9 Madonna and child. Canvas, 43×31 cm. Bergamo, Accademia Carrara. Donated to the Accademia Carrara in 1851 by Conte Marenzi. Kristeller, Fiocco and Tietze ascribe it to after Mantegna's arrival in Mantua; Cipriani to the Paduan period and Paccagnini to after the Mezzarota portrait.

10-11 St Sebastian. Panel, 68×30 cm. Vienna, Kunsthistorisches Museum. Listed in 1659 in the collection of the Archduke Leopold Wilhelm, and passed from his collection to the Museum. Signed on the pilaster in Greek: TO EPTON TOY ANΔPEOY (the work of Andrea). This painting is generally dated about 1459, at the end of the Paduan period, and is identified with the small work executed for the governor of Padua, Antonio Marcello; the Marchese Ludovico Gonzaga allowed Mantegna to postpone his departure for Mantua until 14 March 1459 in order to finish it.

12-13 Agony in the Garden. Panel, 63×80 cm. London, National Gallery. Acquired from Lord Northbrook in 1894, after various changes of ownership (at the beginning of the seventeenth century it was in the Pamphili-Aldobrandini collection and in 1815 belonged to Cardinal Fesch). One of the rocks is signed OPUS ANDREA MANTEGNA. Identified by Cavalcaselle and Richter as the small painting done for Antonio Marcello in 1459, and attached by almost everyone to the Paduan period (Pallucchini considers it as contemporary with the *San Zeno altarpiece*, Tietze with the first episodes of the St James cycle); Fiocco and Knapp date it about 1464; Davies (in the National Gallery Catalogue) between 1460 and 1470.

14-24 San Zeno altarpiece. Three panels, each, 220×115 cm. Padua, San Zeno. The Madonna is seen enthroned between SS. Peter, Paul, John the Evangelist and Zeno, on the left, and SS. Benedict, Lawrence, Gregory and John the Baptist on the right. The whole painting was removed to France in 1797 by Napoleon, then returned in 1815 but minus the predella, consisting of a *Crucifixion* (*pls 21-23*), 60×90 cm, in the Louvre; an *Agony in the garden* (*pl. 20*), 70×92 cm, in the Musée des Beaux-Arts, Tours; and a *Resurrection* (*pl. 24*), 70×92 cm, also in Tours. According to letters written, to both the abbot of San Zeno and to Mantegna, by the Marchese Ludovico Gonzaga, who was trying to lure the painter to Mantua, it was painted between 1456 and the end of 1459. Mantegna also designed the frame. Kristeller has commented on its derivation from the polyptych painted by Antonio Vivarini and Giovanni d'Alemagna in 1446; Knapp, A. Venturi and Fiocco have more usefully demonstrated its links with Donatello's altarpiece in the Church of the Santo, in Padua.

25 Portrait of Cardinal Ludovico Mazzarota. Panel, 44×33 cm. Gemäldegalerie Berlin-Dahlem. The identification of the sitter is based on a print in *Illustrium Virorum Elogia* by Tomasini (1630), and on various medallions. Tietze ascribes it to the end of the Paduan period, and notes affinities with Donatello's Gattamelata; Fiocco considers that it was painted in Mantua during the Council called there by Pius II from 27 May 1459 to 8 February 1469, in which the Cardinal took part.

26 Portrait of a young bishop. Canvas, 25×17.5 cm. Naples, Museo Nazionale. Attributed to Mantegna by Frizzoni and Kristeller, who thought the subject was Francesco Gonzaga, created a bishop at the age of sixteen. Fiocco identified him as the 'baby bishop', Ludovico Gonzaga, already a bishop at the age of six (see *pl. 36*).

27-30 Triptych. Florence, Uffizi. Central panel: *Adoration of the Magi* (*pl. 27*), concave panel, 76×76.5 cm. Left-hand panel: *Ascension* (*pl. 30*), 86×42.5 cm. Right-hand panel: *Circumcision* (*pls 28-29*), 86×42.5 cm. The three paintings were part of the collection of Don Antonio Medici at Valle Muggia near Pistoia in 1587, and in 1632 passed into the Medici collection in Florence. They were arranged as a triptych in a modern frame in 1827, but their original location remains a mystery. Kristeller, Yriarte and Venturi regard them as being the paintings for the chapel of the palace in Mantua mentioned by Vasari ('a small painting showing different stories, the figures not very large, but exquisite'); Mantegna probably painted them at Goito in 1464, because in a letter to the Marchese Ludovico dated 26 April 1464 he mentions certain 'panels' intended for the chapel. Fiocco rejects this identification because, as he points out, the paintings for the chapel were quoted as still being *in situ* in 1657 by Scannelli, whereas the three paintings in question were by that time already in the Medici collection; Fiocco suggests that the paintings were executed during Mantegna's sojourn in Tuscany, in 1466. The problem is complicated by the fact that the panel showing the *Death of the Virgin* in the Prado, according to Longhi's deduction, when completed by the missing upper part (see note to *pl. 31*), corresponds exactly in size to the *Ascension* and the *Circumcision* and would seem to be a partner to them; Longhi in fact partners it with the *Ascension* rather than the *Circumcision*. Tietze does not accept that the triptych was painted for the Mantuan chapel. It is almost impossible to establish a precise chronology for the various parts of the triptych and the matching panel in the Prado; all are works of the highest quality but almost certainly painted with some other disposition in mind. On stylistic grounds the paintings date from between 1460 and 1470.

31-32 Death of the Virgin. Panel, 54×42 cm. Madrid, Prado. The painting appears to have been acquired by Charles I of England in 1627 from the Gonzaga collection in Mantua (Charles's seal is on the back); from England it went to Spain and from 1829 was in the Prado. It is almost certainly Mantuan in origin, although it appears in 1586-8 amongst paintings restored by Bastiano Filippi in the chapel of the Castello in Ferrara. The part showing Christ carrying the Virgin's soul to heaven (not shown) was missing but was traced by Longhi (1934) to the Vendeghini collection in Ferrara and this permitted an exact reconstruction. The fact that the painting was painted in Mantua is proved by the landscape, showing the Ponte di San Giorgio which joins the city of Mantua to the village of San Giorgio on the opposite bank of the river. Only Venturi (in *L'Arte*, 1924) rejects it as being by Mantegna and ascribes it instead to Giovanni Bellini. The painting has been compared with the mosaic of the same subject in the Mascoli chapel, in St Mark's, Venice: Fiocco considers this to have been done by Mantegna in about 1454; Longhi attributed it to a later follower. The *Death of the Virgin* was painted near the beginning of Mantegna's time in Mantua.

33 St George. Panel, 66×33 cm. Venice, Accademia. Acquired in 1856 from the Manfrin collection. Restored by Pelliccioli in 1955. Critics are not in agreement over the date. Tietze, followed by Cipriani, refers it to the Paduan period; Kristeller and Venturi to just after the San Zeno altarpiece; Cavalcaselle to the same period as the Uffizi Triptych; I follow Sandra Moschini, Pallucchini and Fiocco in preferring a later date.

34-35 St Sebastian. Canvas, 257×142 cm. Paris, Louvre. Possibly given by Chiara Gonzaga on her marriage in 1481 to the consul of Aigueperse, from whom it came to the Louvre. Fiocco includes it in the Paduan period, but I prefer to place it later, near the period of the frescoes in the Camera degli Sposi.

36-51 The Camera degli Sposi. Length of each wall 807 cm; height 600 cm; height of the central dome 695 cm. Mantua, Castello di San Giorgio. The square room in the medieval part of the castle was called the Camera Picta in documents; Ridolfi first called it the Camera degli Sposi in 1648. It was probably used as a dining-room. Mantegna's decorations were finished in 1474, according to the inscription on the door of the left-hand wall, but it is not known when they were begun. Various dates have been suggested: 1468 (the date is scratched on the squinch of one of the windows); 1471 (Luzio, Fiocco), 1473 (Tietze), but probably Mantegna started work after the formal visit to Mantua of Cardinal Francesco Gonzaga, in August 1472, referred to in the scene on the left-hand wall. The designs occupy two adjoining walls, divided by imitation columns and painted curtains, which continue the pattern of the real gilded leather hangings on the unpainted walls. The corbels of the dome are supported by the imitation columns; the dome is decorated all over with exquisite imitation plaster moulding, with mythological figures on the vaults and medallion busts of emperors in the lunettes (Tietze compares these decorations with the decorations in the Ducal Palace in Urbino by Laurana). In the centre of the dome, in a large square there is a circular balustrade giving on to the sky, and against the balustrade lean figures and putti (*pls 49-51*). It may have been the technique used by Mantegna, partly on dry plaster (the wall with *The Meeting* and most of the dome were painted on wet plaster, the Court, the lunette and the garland around the opening in the ceiling in tempera on dry plaster), but the paintings deteriorated so rapidly that the first restoration was necessary in 1506, the year of Mantegna's death. They were restored again in the eighteenth and nineteenth centuries. Mauro Pelliccioli restored them to their original state in 1939.

Left-hand wall: *The Meeting (pls 36-40, 42, 43)* between Ludovico Gonzaga and his son Cardinale Francesco, who came to Bondanello 24 August 1472 to have the title of Sant'Andrea conferred upon him. On the left are members of the family holding the horse and dogs belonging to the Marchese; the Marchese is stepping forward into the right-hand compartment towards his son, the Cardinal, standing still in the middle. The cardinal is holding the hand of the ' baby bishop ' (see *pl. 26*) of the Gonzaga household, Ludovico (Tietze identifies the young figure as Pico della Mirandola at the age of nine), and he in his turn is holding the hand of a young cardinal-to-be, Sigismondo, son of Federico. Behind him and next to the Marchese is Gianfrancesco, Federico's eldest son, who later married Isabella d'Este and was the fourth Marchese, from 1484 to 1519. The eldest son, Federico, who succeeded Ludovico in 1478, can be seen in profile in the foreground on the right. The other figures (not identified) standing between the cardinal and Federico may include the court painters; it has been suggested that the character facing the spectator is Mantegna himself. Over the door in the central compartment a group of putti hold up Mantegna's dedication tablet *(pl. 41)*. Right-hand wall: *The Court (pls 44-8)*. The only characters identified with any certainty here are the Marchese Ludovico and his consort Barbara of Brandenburg *(pl. 44)*.

The Triumph of Caesar. Black and white illustration on p. 37. Series of nine panels. Tempera on canvas, 274×274 cm. London, Hampton Court Palace. Detail. Vasari claims that the cycle was completed for Ludovico Gonzaga, but documents show that Mantegna was working on it from August 1486 until February 1492: it was probably finished in 1492 though two panels which were part of the whole were never in fact completed. The work was spread over a number of years and broken off during Mantegna's trip to Rome in 1488-90. After the painter's death in 1506 the nine panels were housed in the painter's house at San Sebastiano, but they were brought back to the palace in the early seventeenth century and remained there until they were acquired in 1629 by Charles I of England. The many moves and repaintings caused almost total deterioration which the attempts made at restoration in 1911 and 1930 could not really remedy; the original structure and colour scheme can only really be guessed. *The Triumph* has been the subject of much speculation. One of the literary sources that appears to have been fundamental is Valturio's *De re militari,* published in Verona in 1472.

The Triumph of Caesar (see p. 36)

52 The Virgin of the Stonecutters (Madonna delle Cave).
Panel, 29×21.5 cm. Florence, Uffizi. This painting was seen by
Vasari in the collection of Francesco de' Medici in Florence; he gives
a detailed description of it, and claims that it was painted by
Mantegna during his Roman period, that is between 1488 and
1490. Yriarte and Venturi support Vasari's theory, but Knapp
and Fiocco attribute the work to 1466 (when Mantegna was in
Tuscany), and Kristeller to sometime later. Tietze, though she accepts
the date 1490, introduces the possibility that the painting was one
of those given by Mantegna to Lorenzo de' Medici in 1484;
Mantegna mentions the gift in a letter to the Duke written in August
1484, though none of the paintings was listed in the inventory of
Medici possessions made in 1492. The stonecutters in the background
are said to be either the marble cutters at Carrara (Knapp) or those
at Monte Bolca, near Ronca, between Vicenza and Verona.

53 Virgin and Child with cherubim. Panel, 89×71 cm. Milan, Brera Gallery. Acquired by the Brera Academy in 1808 from the church of Santa Maria Maggiore in Venice, where the guides used to cite it as the work of Giovanni Bellini. Only after its restoration in 1885 was it attributed to Mantegna. It is fairly unanimously recognized as the painting described in the 1493 inventory of the d'Este collection, painted for Eleanor of Aragon in 1485.

54-57 Our Lady of Victory (Madonna della Vittoria). Canvas, 280×166 cm. Paris, Louvre. The saints are John the Baptist, Michael, George, Andrew, Longinus and Elizabeth, and the donor is Marchese Francesco Gonzaga. The painting was commissioned by the Marchese after the victory over the French at Fornovo on 6 July 1495, as a gift to the little church built for the occasion, to designs by Mantegna, near Sant'Andrea in Mantua. The painting was hung with great ceremony in 1496 and remained in the church until it was sacked by the French in 1797.

59 Virgin and Child with St John the Baptist and St Mary Magdalene. Canvas, 138×116.5 cm. London, National Gallery. Signed ANDREAS MANTINIA C. P. F. In the seventeenth century the painting was in the possession of Cardinal Cesare Monti, archbishop of Milan; it then passed into the Roverselli collection and came to London in 1855. It is datable around 1500.

59-60 Virgin and Child with cherubim, saints and angels. Canvas, 287×214 cm. Milan, Castello Sforzesco. On the book held by the angel at the bottom is the inscription A. MANTINIA PI. AN. GRACIE 1497, 15 AUGUSTI. Painted for the church of Santa Maria in Organo in Verona, where it remained until it was acquired for the Trivulzio collection in Milan, and thence passed to the gallery where it now is. It has recently been restored by Pellìccioli. Tietze sees a link between the figure of St John the Baptist and the engraving Schongauer B54.

61 Christ seated on a sarcophagus. Panel, 83×51 cm. Copenhagen, Statens Museum for Kunst. Signed ANDREAS MANTINIA, in gold lettering on the base of the sarcophagus. During the eighteenth century it belonged to Cardinal Valenti, secretary to Benedict XIV. Stylistically it belongs to the same period as the *St Sebastian* in Ca' d'Oro, Venice; Tietze dates it 1490, Pallucchini somewhere between 1490 and 1500. Borenius published two woodcuts using the same composition with variations.

62-63 The Dead Christ. Canvas, 68×81 cm. Milan, Brera. Almost unanimously identified as the '*Christ foreshortened*' quoted in 1506 with a *Triumph of Scipio* and *St Sebastian* (see note to *pl. 64*) in Mantegna's studio, in a letter from Ludovico Mantegna to the Marchese. It came into the possession of Cardinal Sigismondo Gonzaga, then in 1630 passed to Cardinal Mazzarino in Rome, thence to France; it was acquired by the Brera in 1824. But a similar work was offered to the King of France by Camillo Pamphili in 1665. Yriarte assigns the painting to Mantegna's Paduan period; Kristeller to the years immediately preceding the Camera degli Sposi; Fiocco to a little after. Fiocco then changed his mind and agreed with Berenson and Tietze that it was a late work. Tietze however, in collaboration with H. Tietze (1941), considers that the Christ in the Brera is only a copy, that the original is a painting in the collection of J. M. Heimann, New York, and that this was painted during Mantegna's sojourn in Florence. In the New York *Christ* the two weeping figures, condemned by Tietze as a graceless insertion, do not appear.

64 St Sebastian. Canvas, 210×91 cm. Venice, Ca' d'Oro. The masterpiece of Mantegna's later years. Dated by Tietze at the time of *The Triumph of Caesar* (1486-92), and by Pallucchini at the very end of the century. Fiocco considers it ' the greatest achievement of what may be described as the master's linear metaphysics '.

65 Judith. Pen and wash, 36×24 cm. Florence, Uffizi. One of Mantegna's best drawings. Several copies exist. Signed vertically on the right ANDREA MANTINIA MCCCCLXXXXI FEBI. Identified as the drawing possessed by Vasari; Berenson and Tietze have demonstrated however that it does not correspond technically with Vasari's description.

66-72 Parnassus. Canvas, 160×192 cm. Paris, Louvre. This and the following canvas belong to the series of allegorical paintings commissioned by Isabella d'Este to decorate the Studiolo in her apartment in the castle in Mantua. She seems to have given very precise instructions about the subject matter. The remaining three canvases of the series are in the Louvre and they depict *Comus,* begun by Mantegna and finished by Lorenzo Costa, an *Allegory* by Lorenzo Costa, and *Chastity* by Perugino. The *Parnassus* (listed in an inventory of 1542 under the more descriptive title of ' Mars and Venus in a moment of pleasure, with Vulcan, and Orpheus playing, and nine dancing Nymphs ') was probably the earliest of the series to be finished as it was already hung in the Studiolo on 3 July 1497. It was acquired by Cardinal Richelieu in 1630 and passed to the Louvre 1801.

73-79 Minerva expelling the Vices from the Grove of Virtue. Canvas, 160×192 cm. Paris, Musée du Louvre. Painted, like the preceding canvas, for Isabella's study, and finished in November 1502; it was then called *The Triumph of Virtue,* but this was rectified by Förster on discovering the scroll around the olive tree in human form, the *Mater Virtutum* who invokes gods and cardinal virtues to chase away vice from her kingdom. According to Paccagnini (1961) the allegory echoes the humanist polemics of the *Hypnerotomachia Poliphili* (published in Venice in 1499); the arboreal architecture and humanized plants can be found there as well.

5 –

4

3

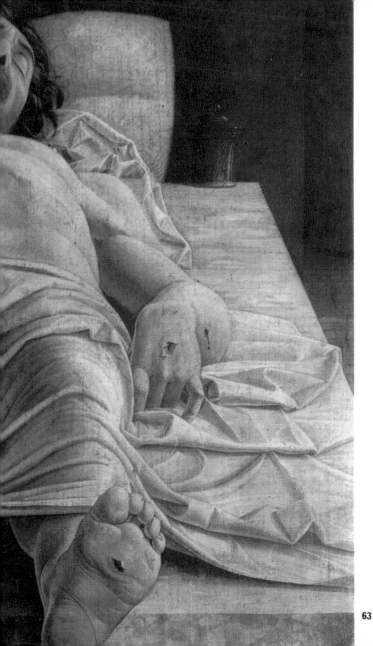